GW00357186

Gardening

WITH THE EXPERTS

ROSES

Gardening
WITH THE EXPERTS

ROSES

BRUCE HARKNESS

Bloomsbury Books
London

Photographs: Kevin Burchett courtesy Weldon Trannies: opposite title page, pages 34, 39.
Ray Joyce courtesy Weldon Trannies: page 16.
Mary Moody: pages 6, 10 (below), 11, 12, 13, 14, 15, 17, 20, 24, 27, 28, 29, 30, 32, 36, 44, 46.
Manuel Patty: pages 40, 41, 42, 43, 45.
Tony Rodd courtesy Weldon Trannies: page 33.
Weldon Trannies: front cover, pages 8, 9, 10 (above), 14, 25.

Published by Harlaxton Publishing Ltd
2 Avenue Road, Grantham, Lincolnshire, NG31 6TA, United Kingdom.
A Member of the Weldon International Group of Companies.

First published in 1990 (Limp)
Reprint 1991 (Cased)
Reprint 1992 (Cased)

This edition published in 1993 by
Bloomsbury Books
an imprint of
The Godfrey Cave Group
42 Bloomsbury Street, London. WC1B 3QJ
under license from Harlaxton Publishing Ltd.

Publishing Manager: Robin Burgess
Illustrations: Kathie Baxter Smith
Typeset in UK by Seller's, Grantham
Produced in Singapore by Imago

British Library Cataloguing-in-Publication data.
A catalogue record for this book is available from the British Library.
Title: Gardening with the Experts: Roses.
ISBN:1 85471 176 8

CONTENTS

INTRODUCTION

Roses are cherished by many a gardener. The flower symbolises numerous events, so this plant has stood the test of time. Roses continue to be popular garden plants.

Fossilised roses found in Europe, Japan and America are reputed to be 35 million years old, but the first pictorial evidence we have is a six petalled flower on a fresco that has been heavily restored at Knossos in Crete, dating back to 1500 BC.

When I began my career as a gardener I had never really liked roses but, like many things in life, as I became familiar with them my interest slowly grew.

Many a plant in the botanical world has its beautiful flowers, perfume and shape, but so often the flowering period is limited. This can be an advantage since, like the seasons, one looks forward to these times. However, the rose is a plant that produces many delightful flowers over such a long season, year after year.

Whether for display purposes or for picking, this ornamental can produce the goods. Many people shy away from growing roses, assuming that one has to implement major spray and fertiliser programmes to achieve good results. In fact, the rose bush (otherwise known as the bush rose), is an extremely hardy plant that will even survive total neglect.

With a little care and attention, these plants can become strong, healthy-looking bushes with attractive blooms.

Page opposite: Roses in a traditional cottage garden.

ROSE TYPES

Roses fall into the following main groups: hybrid teas, floribundas, ramblers and climbers, shrubs and miniatures. Except for ramblers, climbers and standard roses, these groups are usually referred to as bush roses.

HYBRID TEAS

These flower singly or in small clusters. There is often only one flower per stem, For this reason, hybrid teas are sometimes preferred by home gardeners as the blooms look very attractive as cut flowers. Two of

my favourite hybrid teas are 'Fragrant Cloud'® and 'Rosenthal'.

These are very fragrant red roses which look superb in an elegant vase - a must for the table if guests are expected.

FLORIBUNDAS

Floribundas have many flowers on one stem. Because of their cluster-flowering they are very suitable for mass planting and are sometimes used as hedges. One floribunda that looks excellent as a hedge or

Page opposite: A climbing rose. Above: Floribunda roses.

greatly improved through breeding with
hybrid teas. The bushes are more vigorous,
individual flowers are larger and clusters
are more open, with fewer flowers. Some of
these improved floribundas are advertised
as grandiflora roses.

RAMBLERS

Although these are climbing roses, because
they are lax and tractable they can also be
grown horizontally. They can be trained
along low fences or allowed to sprawl over
the ground, ending up as a ground cover.

mass planting is the extremely healthy,
forever-flowering 'Iceberg'®. Another very
recent and popular floribunda that blooms
extremely well is 'Sexy Rexy'®.

Recently some floribundas have been

The main difference between climbers
and ramblers is that growth of climbers is
stiffer and more erect while ramblers are
lax. One of the best-known ramblers and a

Top: A hybrid tea rose.   *Above: 'Dorothy Perkins', a popular rambler.*

10

favourite of mine is 'Albertine'. This rose is free-flowering, vigorous and looks effective on low or high fences, trellises or pergolas.

CLIMBERS

Climbing roses are grown to cover garage walls, neighbours' fences, pergolas, usually to make an attractive feature.

These climbers have many leaders, by tying and pruning them, many laterals will branch off and produce blooms. More vigorous climbers will cover five to six metres while shorter types will have a two metre spread. Shorter types are sometimes known as pillar roses.

In a situation where a vigorous climber is flowering freely on an overhead pergola, a pillar rose can be planted beside the pillar support to give a fuller flowering effect lower down.

SHRUBS

This group covers an exceptionally wide range of modern hybrids of the species (the species are wild roses) and includes all the older types of garden roses often referred to as "old-fashioned" roses.

Old-fashioned roses have shown a real resurgence in recent years, and no wonder. They are naturally almost disease-free and have a wonderful charm all of their own, their history is fascinating, their petal form is extremely varied and many have an exquisite perfume.

A miniature rose 'Rise 'n' Shine'.

11

Their names alone are intriguing. 'Cardinal de Richelieu', 'Duchesse de Montebello', 'Félicité Parmentier', 'Frau Dagmar Hastrupp', 'Honorine de Brabant', 'La Reine Victoria', 'Souvenir de la Malmaison' and 'Souvenir d'un Ami' are just some of the names that immediately conjure thoughts of the grand old gardens spread throughout western Europe.

In fact, it was Napoleon's wife, the Empress Josephine, who helped bring the rose to the forefront among popular garden plants. Early in the nineteenth century she gathered in her garden at Malmaison near Paris, one of the largest collections of roses, to include wild species and garden forms with hybrids. From there the old-fashioned roses were developed further, right up to the modern-day rose.

MINIATURES

A miniature, as the name suggests, is a very small rose, often no higher than 100 mm when planted. Miniatures can be planted in a bed, amongst other rose bushes, as a low border or individually. Miniatures can also be grown in pots or window boxes or even in rockeries.

Miniature roses budded onto standard rootstocks are fast gaining favour. These are standard miniature roses. Two miniature weeping standard roses I like are 'Snow Carpet'® and 'The Fairy'. These roses, planted in clay pots, make attractive plants in a courtyard.

An old-fashioned rose, 'Honorine de Brabant'.

CHOOSING THE RIGHT ROSES

Basically, you need to decide whether you want a mass planting of roses, a mixture of plants, or roses to cover a bare wall.

Naturally there are many choices and combinations that blend in very successfully. What you must avoid, for instance, is growing shorter roses behind high bushes, planting too closely together or placing roses in totally unsuitable conditions.

ROSE BEDS

JUST ROSES

If you possess a very large garden, separate beds containing the same variety of rose (a minimum of nine to eighteen plants) looks extremely attractive. These beds can be square with nine plants, or rectangular with eighteen. I have encountered rectangular beds with a taller variety planted down the middle and lower varieties on either side. This can look quite effective.

Larger plantings of roses are highlighted if the plants are evenly spaced and are surrounded by a beautifully kept expanse of green lawn. Even one large rose bed looks exquisite in a sea of green.

In a small garden a long, narrow bed can be filled with bush roses, interplanted with standard roses towards the back. Standard roses give height at the rear of the planting, while bush roses give bulk and support to the stock onto which the standard roses are budded.

Weeping standards and miniature weeping standards on their own can look

Mixed planting.

13

good, but rows of standards as an edging to a pathway, driveway or against a house with no other supporting vegetation looks absolutely stark and unimaginative.

MIXED PLANTING

Some bush roses go very well in combination with perennial plants. In terraced gardens three, five or seven roses planted some 750 mm to 900 mm apart with plants such as *Nicotiana*, *Lavendula* or *Alyssum* can look quite effective.

The cottage garden is very popular now and can look extremely attractive. Given the space, old-fashioned roses make an ideal backdrop to one of these gardens. An edging of lavender (*Lavandula stoechas*) or English box in the foreground, annuals and

perennials, then add old-fashioned roses or weeping standards, or a combination of these, sets the perfect scene for a hot sunny summer's day.

CLIMBING ROSES

Climbers can be used for many situations, on a fence as a background to a rose bed, covering archways, growing up through dead or living trees, or against buildings.

When selecting a climber, be sure it is the type you require. Some have beautiful blooms but only flower part of the season. Choose varieties that are repeat-flowering unless you want a particular variety and know that it does not repeat. Two healthy, vigorous and repeat flowering climbers are 'Compassion' and 'Dublin Bay'®.

Page opposite: A bed of roses. Above: A climber covers a fence.

POSITION AND SOIL

SUNSHINE
Roses are happiest in a sunny position, the less shade the better. I have often observed roses planted under trees or being rapidly taken over by neighbouring plants. Roses under trees look pitiful. Not only is there a lack of sunshine, but the rose's roots get very dry as they compete for moisture with the tree roots that have invaded the rose root zone.

AIR CIRCULATION
Roses like good air circulation but dislike draughts. Shelter them from strong winds and avoid draughty or static air conditions.

DRAINAGE
Roses will not thrive in poorly drained soil. They dislike being waterlogged for any length of time.

SOIL
Roses will grow in any type of soil provided it is prepared correctly. Roses grow best in soils with a pH of between 5.8 and 6.5.

The aftercare of the soil, once the roses are established, plays an important role in their health and vigour.

Page opposite: Roses thrive in rich humus soil.   Above: Roses prefer a sunny position.

PREPARING FOR PLANTING

ADDING DRAINAGE

If drainage is a major problem in an area that you have chosen for your new rose bed, then a drainage system is required to remove excess water.

A channel dug below the level of the rose bed and leading away from the area is a simple solution. Place clay field pipes or perforated plastic pipes in the channel, then cover them with 20 mm drainage chip (metal chips) to a depth of about 150 mm. To reduce costs exclude the pipes and only use drainage chips, since water will filter through the chips and follow the natural drainage path.

If there is no suitable outflow for a drain, dig a deep soak pit at the channel outlet. Fill this with rocks and/or drainage chips. The water will slowly drain from this sump.

Another solution to drainage problems is to slightly raise the level of the rose beds. Water will run off to the lowest edges and eventually drain away.

SOIL PREPARATION

Humus (decomposed organic matter) rich soil is excellent for plants, including roses. If possible prepare soil some months before planting to allow organic matter to break down and the soil to settle. Autumn is a good time to do this.

In new residential areas, topsoil might have been removed during construction, consequently new residents inherit a clay soil that is hard, stony, or sandy if near the coast. The quickest solution is to remove poor soil to a depth of 450 mm and replace it with a good quality topsoil.

In a garden with, 150 mm of good topsoil with a very heavy clay underneath, dig out the turf (and keep it) for the rose bed area. Remove the clay to a depth of 450 mm and replace it with topsoil.

An alternative method is to incorporate organic matter into the clay subsoil. With a spade, remove turf along the length of the proposed rose bed, then repeat this so that there are two spade widths removed. This will give room to work. Then dig over the clay subsoil, breaking it down with the spade. Using a border fork, mix plenty of organic matter (to a depth of 100 mm) into the clay. Use mushroom compost, well-rotted compost from refuse bins, sheep or cow manure, pea straw, ordinary straw, or some soil conditioner from a local garden centre. Finally, dig out another row of turf and turn it upside down onto the newly laid organic matter.

If rose beds have not been prepared in advance, then for immediate planting, prepare soil as described above and give it a good "heeling over". That is, after compost has been mixed in, walk systematically

Page opposite: A raised garden bed.

over the bed with the heels of your boots. Then rake it over. This will ensure that the newly dug bed does not settle down at a later date. Do not heel over when the soil is very wet, since valuable air pockets will be lost and soil texture will suffer, creating a pudgy soil.

ADDING NUTRIENTS

Once beds have been dug over, give them a light dressing of lime or dolomite to reduce soil acidity.

Although roses like soil to be slightly acid, new soil or old, exhausted garden soil will benefit from this application. Soil that is fairly acidic binds necessary nutrients. Dolomite and lime, by reducing soil acidity makes these nutrients readily available.

Ordinary lime is calcium carbonate.

Dolomite is calcium magnesium carbonate and is more beneficial as it adds magnesium to the soil which helps maintain a suitable balance between levels of magnesium and calcium. Gently fork the dolomite or lime into the top 100 mm of soil.

Prior to planting roses, apply a light dressing of blood and bone to the soil with superphosphate if desired. Personally, I prefer to feed my roses about a month after planting. I feel they need time to adjust to their new environment, after which they are able to make full use of nutrients that leach down to their root zone.

RECEIVING NEW ROSES

After buying new roses in winter from a garden centre or having them delivered by mail, make sure that roots are kept moist at

Receiving new roses.

all times.

Allowing roots to dry out is a major cause of losses. Roses should be planted as soon as possible after getting them home. Grower digs them out to meet orders for late autumn. While potted stock is very convenient, bare-rooted specimens make it easier to inspect the root stock. Often they are packed in sawdust or with wet, shredded paper around the root zone. After a while roots dry out, so if you do not intend to plant them straight away, remove the packing and heel your roses into a vacant plot. Just dig a trench, place the roses, then cover the roots with soil and heel them in.

SPACING

When several roses are being planted in large beds, it is essential to mark out each rose's future position with a small stake or bamboo stick. Otherwise with uneven spacing they will have to be dug out and started again. For vigorous bush roses one pace from the bush centre is ample space.

PRUNING NEW ROSES

Contrary to popular belief, new roses have not usually been pruned by nurserymen, only trimmed for ease of handling, packing, transporting and for general appearance at the point of sale in the store.

Often a rose grower will zoom along rows of "ready to be sold" roses with an electric cutter, so that all the branches are cut to the same height.

Before planting roses, remove all thin, spindly branches and any soft, immature shoots, to retain a framework of strong, healthy branches.

Prune just above a strong bud, preferably one that points outwards to consider the eventual overall shape of the trained plant. The centre of the plant will be a void to encourage air circulation and sunlight.

Bush roses should be pruned back to approximately 130 mm from the crown (see page 22 "Planting Day"), try to leave about three or four buds on each branch.

Thin out surplus shoots and shorten stems to the first good bud from the top.

Climbers should be pruned back to a height of approximately 300 mm and standard roses to between 150 to 200 mm from the crown.

AVERAGE SPACING

MINIATURES	300 mm
LOW, COMPACT BUSH ROSES	450 mm
AVERAGE-SIZED ROSES	750 mm
VIGOROUS VARIETIES	1 metre
CLIMBERS	3 metre

(allow more for very vigorous varieties)

STANDARDS	minimum 1.2 metre

PLANTING DAY

Roses can be planted at almost any time, depending on whether the plant is bare-rooted or potted. From late autumn over winter during suitable weather, until spring is most usual.

If the soil is fairly dry and the sun is out, then this is a good day to plant. Keep the rose roots wet at all times. Once removed from their heeled-in position, soak roots in a bucket of water. If roots are split, partially broken, or damaged then cut them back to where the root is intact.

Most rose varieties are budded onto Rosa multiflora rootstock. (Multiflora rootstock is a strong and vigorous old briar rose).

Rose growers prefer to use this method rather than taking cuttings as the former produces a far greater and faster yield with a stronger root system.

The point at which the roots meet the budded variety is known as the 'budhead', 'crown' or 'union'.

When a new rose is planted consider two points, climatic severity and future spring mulching. In warm regions, this budhead should show just above the surface of the soil to allow for future mulching adding to the soil level. In cool regions, because of the risk of frost damage, the crown should be set just below the soil surface, but when mulching in future, ensure that the surface is even since a depression will gather water, seep down to the rootstock and cause rot.

This raises a further consideration when buying roses. Try to choose roses that have

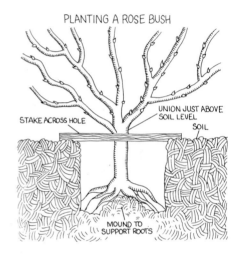

PLANTING A ROSE BUSH

STAKE ACROSS HOLE
UNION JUST ABOVE SOIL LEVEL
SOIL
MOUND TO SUPPORT ROOTS

been budded fairly close to the roots, that is, no more than 150 mm above the root zone. When roses have been budded higher than this, to plant them with the bud union just above ground level, roots need to be buried to a greater depth, where they may not receive water and nutrients as efficiently as those closer to the surface.

Dig a round hole in the rose bed with a small mound in the centre to support the root system. The hole size should suit the root system and height of the budhead. Never curl roots around to fit the hole. If roots are too long prune them back, as described above. Place roots on the mound and see if the depth of the hole is correct.

A small stake laid across the hole will aid to determine if the budhead is above or below the soil surface. Once roots are sat at the correct height, splay them evenly around the mound. Then begin to cover the roots, work fine soil between and over roots, firming it down as you go.

Standard roses are planted in much the same way, but a supporting stake should be driven in before planting to avoid damage to the root system.

After planting, use soft bands of sack webbing or old stockings to tie stems of the standard rose firmly to the stake so that there is no rubbing when the wind blows.

I wrap webbing twice around the stake (to prevent chafing the stem) and then wrap around the stem twice. Secure the webbing with two or three small flat-head nails driven through the webbing into the wooden stake, or by threading strong twine through holes in the webbing and tying it around the stake.

Climbers are planted like bush roses, but they should be brought out a minimum of 100 mm from any wall or pergola support so that they can be leaned slightly towards the support when planted.

This will make it easier to train the direction of new leaders than if the plant is placed hard against its future support.

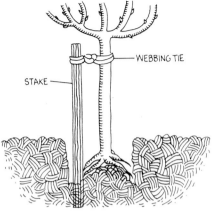

PLANTING A STANDARD

PLANTING A CLIMBER

23

PRUNING

EQUIPMENT

Secateurs with the parrot-beak type blades are needed, as well as loppers for thick, old branches. A pruning saw is sometimes needed to deal with larger branches and to remove stubs or branches close to the budhead, which loppers and secateurs are unable to reach. Gardening gloves are also needed to protect hands.

BUSH ROSES

In mild areas pruning can be done in autumn or early spring, in areas subject to hard frosts final pruning is best left until early spring to avoid frost damage to young, tender growth.

If modern bush roses are not pruned, they will eventually become straggly, carry a lot of dead wood, produce fewer blooms, become diseased and finally regress.

An analogy I like to use is, if we allow our hair to grow long it eventually develops split ends and grows less vigorously. A good trim every so often improves the shape and speeds growth. Roses are similar, an annual winter prune during the dormant period rejuvenates these bushes. Pruning assists natural methods of replacing old, unproductive stems with new and vigorous ones. Each summer most roses, if well fed, will develop new canes from the budhead.

DEAD AND OLD WOOD

The first thing to remove from your bush is all dead wood, weak or straggly branches, and old canes that carry only thin shoots, as far as is practical. You should aim to retain a minimum of three to five canes on an established rose bush, so always cast an eye over the whole bush before pruning. That is, do not cut out all the old wood if there is no new wood to replace it.

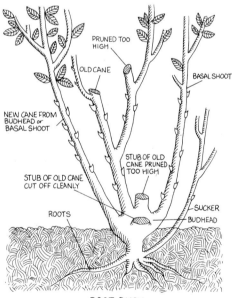

ROSE BUSH

Page opposite: Modern bush roses require pruning.

When pruning these dead and old canes, make cuts as close as possible to the budhead. You may need to scrape back soil or mulch to saw off old canes flush with the budhead. Any cane stub that is left on the budhead will be a potential harbour for future disease.

REMOVING CENTRAL WOOD

Remove canes that are going to grow across the centre of the bush, ones that are too close to others, or stems that are crossing. Crossing canes will rub against each other, causing scars that may weaken and snap to allow infection to enter the plant.

The reasons for removing central wood, or as much as is feasible are, to have an open bush that allows light to penetrate and air to circulate, also to persuade new stems to grow outwards away from the centre of the bush.

Incidentally, at first new wood or canes are often reddish brown, only later do they become a healthy smooth green bark. As branches age to four to five years old, they will tend to turn greyish brown with the bark texture becoming rough and lined.

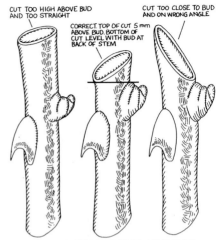

CUT TOO HIGH ABOVE BUD AND TOO STRAIGHT

CORRECT TOP OF CUT 5 mm ABOVE BUD, BOTTOM OF CUT LEVEL WITH BUD AT BACK OF STEM

CUT TOO CLOSE TO BUD AND ON WRONG ANGLE

METHOD OF MAKING PRUNING CUTS

PRUNING BACK

Think of the ideal pruned rose bush as an open vase shape with a minimum of five healthy, young canes pruned with buds facing outward approximately 230 mm from the ground. This is the ideal picture. However, roses seldom grow by the book.

Having removed all the unwanted wood, you now need to reduce the new canes to approximately 230 mm above the ground.

Close inspection of a healthy rose stem, will show little buds which appear around the stem at regular intervals from its base.

Under each bud is a horizontal line that is known as the leaf scar. These dormant buds, sometimes known as eyes or shoots, are the points of pruning cuts.

Once a suitable outward direction facing bud has been found (seldom do all canes have buds facing outwards at the desired height), make a cut about 5 mm above the bud at a 45 degree angle. A cut in this way will help water run off the cut cane and take it away from the bud where it may otherwise cause damage.

HARD PRUNED

PRUNING BASAL SHOOTS

Basal shoots, or "water shoots" as they are often called, because of their soft, lush growth, are usually not hard enough to prune back during early summer nor do they have buds lower down on their stems.

In cold climates they should be removed because they are regularly damaged by frost. In warmer regions, try to keep these water shoots since they are the best wood on the bush for the future.

Treat the flower head (which is a cluster on short stems) as if deadheading. That is, remove individual flower stems back to the buds. As these canes harden up and mature during the following summer, they become suitable for normal pruning during the following winter.

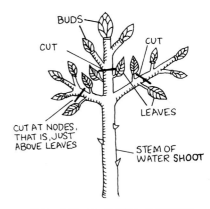

DEADHEADING BASAL SHOOTS

A formal garden with a weeping standard.

HYBRID TEAS AND FLORIBUNDAS

The general rule for hybrid teas is to prune mature bushes moderately, to 230 mm from the ground, but to prune floribundas a little higher.

STANDARD ROSES

Standard roses do not have the same power of regeneration as a bush rose, so do not remove so much growth when pruning. However, the principle is the same - prune to an outward bud, if possible, and try to keep the centre of the bush fairly open.

MINIATURES

Prune miniatures with a light trim all over.

CLIMBERS

Replace as many old canes as possible with new ones. As a rule, on the remaining old canes, prune back side branches (laterals growing off the leader) to the second bud out from the cane. With new canes, reduce the growing tip, that will encourage them to become stronger and shoot out lateral growth from which flowers will bloom. The

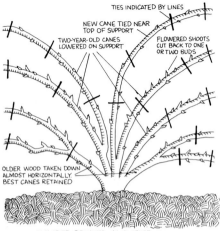

TIES INDICATED BY LINES
NEW CANE TIED NEAR
TOP OF SUPPORT
TWO-YEAR-OLD CANES
LOWERED ON SUPPORT
FLOWERED SHOOTS
CUT BACK TO ONE
OR TWO BUDS
OLDER WOOD TAKEN DOWN
ALMOST HORIZONTALLY.
BEST CANES RETAINED

CLIMBER PRUNED AND TIED IN

old and new canes should be spread out evenly along the support. Climbing roses flower much better if trained horizontally, as they will flower all along the branches instead of just at the tips.

Tie new growth to the support structure and renew old ties. Cut up old stockings make excellent ties for climbers.

Rosa banksiae 'Lutea' is a well-known yellow climber that flowers in early spring. As soon as this climber has flowered, it should be lightly pruned back. If it has been pruned in midwinter very few flowers will bloom the following summer.

RAMBLERS

True ramblers bloom only on wood grown during the previous year. Remove all old canes and prune as soon as flowering has finished. This gives the new shoots better growing conditions for the remainder of the season. After the old canes have been removed, tie in all the new canes. This is usually done in midsummer after flowering is complete.

We always pruned 'Albertine', a rambler,

with hedge clippers. We would first remove only canes that had lost their vigour then tie all the new canes into pergola supports, plus check the ties on existing canes. Once ties were replaced on the pergola frame, we would clip all the laterals with the hedge clippers. This was far quicker for a vigorous well-established rambler like 'Albertine'. A quick removal of dead wood amongst the jumble of laterals, and the job is complete.

OLD FASHIONED ROSES

Many roses in this category, such as *Alba, Centifolia, Damask, Gallica* and *Moss*, need little pruning. After flowering very old wood should be removed to encourage strong, young basal growth. These growths may be shortened by a third in midsummer to avoid wind damage. Besides removing dead and spindly wood, old roses can be pruned to suit your needs. My old roses at home are 1.5 metres high by 1 metre wide.

A miniature such as 'The Fairy' is pruned with a light trim all over.

'Frau Dagmar Hastrupp', an old rose which needs little pruning.

EXCEPTIONS

Some bush roses produce most blooms if pruned lightly, instead of using tradition-ally hard, open vase-shaped methods of pruning. Many of these roses will flower well on pencil-sized pieces of growth, such as 'Iceberg'® which is capable of a larger framework of wood as it is a very vigorous growing and healthy variety.

'Iceberg ' ®

Remove any dead wood and spindly growth then prune back all remaining growth to buds. As a general guide, the retained wood should be the size of a pencil.

A bed of nine 'Iceberg'® roses grown at the Lady Norwood Rose Gardens in Wellington New Zealand, used to reach a height of about 2.5 metres each summer.

Each July I would go with hedge clippers and a little garden stool for elevation to clip this bed of roses into a shape down to approximately 1.5 metres high. Then armed with secateurs I would prune out all dead and spindly wood, reducing any cuts made by the hedge clippers that were too high above a bud. For a well-established individual plant, a hedge, or a bed of 'Iceberg'® roses, this method gives a good shape, is rapid and convenient.

'First Love'

This bush rose does not produce many basal shoots (new canes) so it needs only a light pruning. I prune it using the vase shape system but retain several pencil sized growths off mature canes if new growth is non-existent.

OTHER BUSH ROSES

Some roses such as 'Josephine Bruce', 'Percy Thrower' and 'Europeana'® have a spreading type of growth, often requiring that canes be pruned to an upward facing bud, so as to arrest excessive spread.

SUCKERS

Occasionally a rose will sucker from the multiflora rootstock. If allowed to grow this sucker will eventually dominate the bush.

Suckers are easily identified as they have feathery leaflets of a lighter, dull green. Pull or cut off the sucker with a sliver of rootstock, rather than cut it off above the growth point, as it will continue to shoot.

'Iceberg'® roses can be pruned with hedge clippers.

CULTURAL CARE

When pruning is complete, if time permits cover all pruning cuts on major canes with a pruning paste or vaseline. Even rubbing dirt into cuts will help seal the wounds.

The idea is to prevent fungus spores infecting the rose. Any fresh cut is an ideal entry point. One fatal disease for roses is *silverleaf*. There are many host plants such as cherries and silver birches.

Pick up all dead leaves or pruning debris from the rose bed. Do not compost these, either burn them or take them to a refuse tip. They contain overwintering spores, that if left in the rose beds will infect roses in the spring.

SPRAY PROGRAMME

For a top display of roses a regular spray programme is essential. Having said that, many people spray irregularly or prefer to use organic sprays, yet still achieve good results. Irregular or non-existent spraying is noticeable towards the end of summer when diseases such as rust appear, the rose bush may lose many of its leaves.

During very warm weather, especially in humid climates mildew problems can be quite prevalent.

COMBINATION SPRAYS

There are combination sprays available containing several ingredients that control most pests and diseases. Some are supplied in powder form, some as a liquid. There are

also chemicals suited to mixing in a water solution for spraying, but always check that they are compatible.

Many different sprays contain identical ingredients without the customer realising. To further complicate matters, each chemical has a common name, but a single chemical may be sold under up to ten trade names, depending on who markets the product. Always read the labels on products—it is surprising how much useful information these provide.

There are many, many types of sprays for roses. I am not going to list all those available, only the main groups.

WINTER SPRAYING

After pruning, spray rose plants and beds with a good clean-up winter spray.

I usually spray mine with lime sulphur. *Winter rate:* 1 part lime sulphur to 15 parts water. *Controls:* powdery mildew, black spot, rust, moss, lichen and scale insects.

Another winter spray is made combining copper oxychloride with All Purpose Oil (but not winter oil). *Winter rates:* 25 gm copper oxychloride with 200 ml All Purpose Oil in 5 litres water. *Controls:* copper oxychloride—black spot and downy mildew; All Purpose Oil—rust, scale insects and red mite. *How to mix:* Half fill the sprayer with clean water. Put copper oxychloride (a powder) into a measuring jug and fill it up with water. Stir the mixture thoroughly then pour it into the sprayer. Rinse the jug with water and pour the residue into the sprayer. Pour the All Purpose Oil into jug then fill it up with water. Pour the mixture into the sprayer. Rinse the jug and pour the residue into the sprayer. Then pour the rest of the water into the sprayer.

Always mix powder and liquid chemicals this way.

Some rose lovers spray their roses with lime sulphur before pruning followed by a copper oxychloride-All Purpose Oil spray combination after pruning.

Note: Do not spray with All Purpose Oil within fourteen days of using lime sulphur. These winter application rates are designed for dormant deciduous plant growth only. If they were applied to new growth, the leaves and buds would be burned.

EARLY SPRING SPRAYING

Once roses start to break into leaf growth insect problems are not so apparent, but you still need to keep fungal diseases such as black spot or downy mildew at bay.

Foliage affected by black spot.

In early spring, spray fortnightly with copper oxychloride-25 mg/5 litres of water. *Optional:* The spring rate of All Purpose Oil - 100 ml. added to copper oxychloride solution.

Note: Be careful with oil sprays in the spring as the soft new growth can be damaged by these sprays. I have had good control in early spring with just the copper oxychloride spray.

SUMMER SPRAY PROGRAMME

After the last spring spraying wait for two weeks then commence the main season's spray programme.

From late spring to late autumn spray fortnightly. The main spray I used for ten years at the Lady Norwood Rose Gardens combined four ingredients with 5 litres of water:

1. Dithane -common name Maneb (powder). Contact fungicide.
   Controls: black spot and rust to a degree.
   Rate: 10 gm (10 gm = approximately 4 level teaspoons).
2. Benlate-common name Benomyl (powder). A systemic fungicide with protectant and eradicant properties.
   Controls: powdery mildew and black spot. *Rate:* 2 5 gm. This is an excellent fungicide.
3. All Purpose Oil-common names Sun Spray, Conqueror Oil (liquid).
   Controls: rust, red mite, scale insects and helps smother aphids. Also acts as a wetting agent, that is, it helps other chemicals stick to the plant.
   Rate: 50 ml.
4. Maldison-common name Malathion (liquid). Can also be purchased as a powder. A contact insecticide.
   Controls: aphids, mealy bugs, thrips, leaf-hoppers, caterpillars and beetles.

Rate: 10-15 ml (2-3 teaspoons). I would only add the Malathion if aphids were present on the rose bushes.

Note: Use combination sprays on the same day that they have been mixed. They lose their effectiveness if left to stand for days in the sprayer.

Some ready-made sprays are:
1. Shield -also known as Saprene (liquid). A combination spray for roses and ornamentals. *Controls:* black spot, rust, powdery mildew, aphids and caterpillars. *Rate:* 2 ml/5 litres water. This spray is very popular with home gardeners as it is easy to use and quite effective. There is some doubt whether it controls rust adequately.

2. Rose and Ornamental Spray-(powder). This is a very good combination spray. *Controls:* black spot, rust, beetles, leaf-hoppers, mealy bugs and powdery mildew. *Rate:* 130 gm/5 litres water. Spray fortnightly.
3. General Garden Spray-(powder). This is a spray that you could use on your roses if you already had it at home. *Controls:* beetles, leaf-hoppers, mealy bugs, aphids, thrips, caterpillars, powdery mildew, mite species. *Rate:* 40 gm/5 litres water. Spray fortnightly.
4. Rose Spray-(liquid). A good combination rose spray. *Controls:* mite species, aphids, woolly aphids, thrips, black spot, rust, downy and powdery mildews.

If there is a problem with a fungal disease like rust, one excellent spray to use on its

Insects can be controlled by regular spraying.

Healthy blooms.

own is:

5. Calirus-a systemic fungicide, both a protectant and eradicant. *Rate:* 10 gm/5 litres water. Spray fortnightly. It is **not** compatible with other sprays.

It is worth remembering that it is better to spray regularly to prevent diseases rather than having to cure them.

Resistance to chemicals: With your main summer spray programme it is advisable to alternate the types of chemicals used, since resistance to particular chemicals by plant varieties can develop.

For this reason it is as well to consider the use of alternative remedies or solutions such as derris, dimethoate, dinocap, formothion, nicotine, tar oil, thiram and finally zineb.

Safety with chemicals:

1. Read the label before using.
2. Some chemicals are not compatible with each other. Observe the manufacturer's recommendations.
3. Use clean equipment and clean it thoroughly after use. Avoid equipment that has been used for applying herbicides.
4. Do not spray when foliage is dewy or wet or when it is very windy.
5. Do not eat, drink or smoke when handling chemicals or equipment.
6. Wash hands thoroughly with soap and water after spraying. Wash off immediately with cold water any concentrated chemical that may have splashed onto your skin.

7. Keep chemicals and equipment in a separate locked cupboard when not in use.
8. Destroy empty spray containers.

CULTIVATION AND MULCHING

Winter is an excellent time to weed and gently fork over rose beds. It is easy to move amongst the bushes as there is no new growth which could easily be broken off later.

Gentle forking reduces compact soil created while pruning and allows aeration of the earth. Do not fork too deeply since well-established roses have a multitude of fine feeder roots just under the soil surface.

Once cultivation is completed, cover the rose beds with a suitable mulch. An ideal one is mushroom mulch-the spent medium used for growing mushrooms. This medium usually has a pH of 6.5, exactly as required by roses. Cover beds to a minimum depth of 50 to 75 mm to make it worthwhile, and do not be over concerned about covering the crown of the rose bush.

Benefits of mulching:
1. Reduces weeding. Weeds that do come through are easily pulled out.
2. Keeps soil temperatures even during winter or summer. Roses thrive with a cool root run in summer.
3. Helps the soil retain moisture. With irrigation in drier months, the mulch holds the moisture and helps prevent evaporation.
4. Greatly improves the growing soil. Clay soils - improves texture, structure, drainage and aeration. Lighter, sandy soils - improves their ability to retain nutrients and moisture.
5. Provides plants with trace elements.
6. Encourages more feeder roots to develop so the rose bush will produce more basal shoots each growing season.

Mushroom mulch is a sterilised medium so the rose garden does not inherit any weeds or diseases.

The gardeners of the Lady Norwood Rose Gardens, were once offered free stable manure. Delighted, we spread truckloads of the stuff. Several weeks later thousands of dock seedlings appeared. We removed all the stable manure, then two gardeners very carefully weeded all the docks out. Mulches are meant to reduce labour requirement, but there we increased it! So beware!

Some rose growers use untreated sawdust, straw or grass clippings as mulches. These are satisfactory, but they do initially deplete soil of some nitrogen nor are they aesthetically attractive.

FERTILISING

Once the leaves on your rose bushes are growing well it is time to feed them. With warmer weather the feeder roots begin to grow. A little often is a good rule of thumb.

Rose fertiliser mixture:
3 parts blood and bone
2 parts superphosphate
1 part sulphate of potash
1 part sulphate of magnesium
1 part sulphate of iron

Apply two handfuls of this mixture around the dripline (not against the bush) at the on set of spring followed by two months before the next application, then again two months later. After each application gently hoe it into the mulch or soil.

If you do not want to go to the trouble of making your own mixture, you can buy a ready-made rose fertiliser. These usually have nutrients and proportions similar to the above mixture. If you make up your own mixture for the third application towards autumn, do **not** add the blood and

bone. At this time we want to slow down autumn growth of roses, but it is important to apply fertiliser as the sulphate of potash helps to harden the soft new wood that the bush or climber has produced. It can be disappointing to prune a vigorous young cane in winter only to discover that it is still quite soft and splits when you prune it.

WATERING

Roses respond quite noticeably to irrigation during dry months. A proper watering must soak soil to allow the water to penetrate the mulch and sink well down into the root zone. A general guide for dry spells is thirty to forty-five minutes with a sprinkler covering a whole rose bed. Water roses this' way every third day or about twice a week. Early morning or evening is a good time, as water can fade your blooms, particularly in bright sunshine.

Plenty of water really helps the rose bush to throw up new canes.

One year I recall not watering the roses for about two weeks at the peak of summer. They started to look a little straggly. After two good doses of water the roses perked up considerably, their foliage once again fresh and glossy. But what was more important, was the usual abundance of new wood that began to appear.

You will know when roses have had enough water. Do not overwater since this may leach nutrients from the soil.

DEADHEADING

Winter pruning completed, the initial fertilising completed and a summer spray programme into gear, you await the first flush of spring blooms. There is always the odd bush or variety that opens before the rest, but usually most of your roses will bloom within two weeks of each other. In warmer regions this can be sooner, while in cooler regions, it will be later.

To increase the number of blooms per bush per summer, you must deadhead the bushes regularly. Once a bloom is past its best, prune back to the first strong bud and this bud will produce another bloom or blooms within four to six weeks. This means that by midsummer in most regions there will be a second flush of blooms well under way. Some people say you must cut back to the first bud where five leaflets appear. This is not always so. Certainly there are often very strong buds at this point, but equally often there are just as suitable buds above. When picking roses for a vase, always cut back to a strong bud.

Hybrid Teas

With hybrid teas simply deadhead to a strong bud.

Floribundas

On the cluster-type flower head there may be several spent blooms, several blooms just opening or opened, as well as buds still closed. Simply remove the spent blooms and stalks from the flower head.

Once the complete flower head has bloomed, prune back to the first strong bud. It can be helpful to prune to a slightly outward-facing bud in some instances.

SUMMER PRUNING

In some very strong growing districts, home gardeners have rose bushes that reach to heights of nearly 3 metres. To control these "giants" they reduce them back by a third of their height to a strong bud.

Page opposite: Fertiliser helps to harden new wood produced by bush roses.

SELECTING ROSES TO GROW

When ordering roses from a grower it is as well to confirm their closing dates for new orders by telephone, then mail the written request as early as possible. Late orders can lead to disappointment. Check also that the grower produces what is known as "High Health" roses. Woody crops, such as roses, ornamental trees and fruit trees, are propagated by budding or grafting and tend to accumulate viruses with repeated propagation. Once a plant is infected, all subsequent plants carry this disorder.

In recent years reputable rose nurseries have been selecting their rootstocks and varieties from sources substantially free of known viruses.

Selecting roses is very much a personal affair, but here are but a few of my own personal choices.

BUSH ROSES
(Fl) = floribunda : (HT) = hybrid tea

'Chanelle' (Fl): Perfect HT-shaped flowers of cream and buff, shaded with pink. Very vigorous and bushy, with healthy, dark foliage and plenty of flowers.
'Eroica' (HT): Small, dark velvety crimson flowers with a strong fragrance. A large-growing, healthy bush with lots of foliage.
'First Love' (HT): Very long, elegant buds opening to wide flowers of pale pink with

'Fragrant Cloud'®.

light apricot tonings. Marvellous for floral work, with long, almost thornless stems.
'Fragrant Cloud'® (HT): One of my favourites. The scent is superb. A free flowering bush with a healthy medium height and bright cinnabar-red flowers.
'Iceberg'® (Fl): One of the best of the white floribundas. Grows strongly to a large bush absolutely smothered with long sprays of pure-white flowers, lovely for flower arrangements. Attractive light green foliage and extremely disease resistant .
'Kerryman'® (Fl-HT): Lovely HT flowers of creamy pink with deeper margins. A spreading bush with healthy foliage and a long flowering season. Because this flowers so well, it looks great planted in a mass bed and does well in a container.

Page opposite: 'Maria Callas'.

41

'Kronenbourg'® (HT): Large, well formed blooms of deep velvety claret, with straw yellow on the underside. It is a sort of 'Peace' ® and consequently has all the growth, vigour and form of its parent but a very different colour.

'Maria Callas' (HT): Another one of my favourites. I love large, full bodied blooms of rich carmine-pink and their sweet scent. A vigorous, free flowering bush with large, leathery foliage. Highly resistant to disease.

'Peter Frankenfeldt'® (HT): Long, spiral buds opening to large blooms of luminous cerise-pink with a good petal texture. Free-flowering with blooms ideal for cutting.

'Rosenthal' (HT): Another favourite, as it has tightly curled buds, a beautiful colour and an excellent scent. A dark velvety red with glowing, urn-shaped buds. Keeps well in water when picked.

'Sexy Rexy'® (Fl): An outstanding new rose which is hard to fault. Large, well-spaced trusses of soft-pink blooms with an attractive form. Very free flowering and quick-repeating. Dark green, disease-resistant foliage.

'Western Sun' (HT): Vivid, deep golden-yellow, this rose has always caught my eye. The full flowers, freely borne on stiff stems, are non-fading from bud to petal drop. A sturdy, upright habit with plentiful, light green foliage.

Other bush roses that deserve a mention are: 'Burgundiaca', 'Europeana'®, 'Josephine Bruce', 'Liverpool Echo', 'Madam President', 'Margaret Merril'®, 'Pearl Drift'®, 'Precious Platinum', 'Strawberry Ice', 'Sylvia' and 'Whisky Mac'®.

'Peter Frankenfeldt' ®

42

'Sexy Rexy' ®

CLIMBERS

'Casino'®: Large, soft, yellow blooms of HT form borne over a long period on a healthy plant of medium vigour with light green foliage.

'Compassion': Perfectly formed HT type blooms of salmon-pink shaded with apricot-orange, sweetly perfumed and perfect for cutting. Very vigorous, healthy growth with dark foliage. Repeat-flowering.

'Dublin Bay'®: Clusters of brilliant deep-red, fragrant blooms borne almost continuously. A strong, healthy plant with good foliage. An excellent climber.

'Parkdirektor Riggers'®: Clusters of bright scarlet blooms, well displayed on a large, vigorous plant with abundant, glossy foliage. Always in flower.

'Precious Platinum'.

'Félicité Parmentier'.

'Sylvia'

OLD FASHIONED ROSES

'Cécile Brunner' (*rosa chinensis*): Sweetheart rose. Charming, small, soft-pink flowers. Continuous flowering. Can have climbing and bush varieties.

'Félicité Parmentier' (*alba*): Full, open flowers of soft-pink, highly scented, with grey-green foliage. One of the best albas. Grows to 1 metre.

'Madame Isaac Pereire' (*bourbon*): Large, double flowers of purple-crimson on a big, ranging bush. Very fragrant. I have trained one of these into a pillar rose, 2.5 m high.

'Souvenir de la Malmaison' (*bourbon*): Climbing and bush forms. A beautiful rose of blush-white opening to a flat, quartered shape. Scented and free flowering.

'Souvenir d'un Ami' (*tea*): A vigorous rose with large, double, fragrant flowers of rose-pink. Repeat-flowering. Grows to 1.5 m.

MINIATURE WEEPING STANDARDS

These are ground-cover roses budded onto an 840 mm stem. They make beautiful, small trees which weep right down to the ground and flower throughout the season. They look excellent in pots in courtyards or in a bed that cannot accommodate a full-size weeping standard.

'Snow Carpet'®: Miniature leaves and flowers and a dense, spreading habit of growth. The branches reach the ground and are smothered with dainty, creamy white flowers like a fresh fall of snow.

'The Fairy': Makes a wide-spreading and trailing head with masses of soft pink, rosette-shaped flowers in large clusters. Beautiful, shining, disease-free foliage and a good continuity of flowering.

PATIO ROSES

Over recent years a completely new type of

'Bloomheld Courage', a weeping standard.

bush rose has evolved—the patio or cushion rose. They can be very low growing and compact, or can have a spreading habit. They never reach more than 600 mm, have wonderful flowers and are extremely healthy and easy to grow. They are ideal for paved and patio areas, pots and tubs, and for planting as edgings for beds and borders, on or against low walls and along pathways.

ROSES IN CONTAINERS

For apartment blocks, town-houses and small gardens, roses in tubs make an attractive display. We have five roses in clay tubs in our rear courtyard. They are 'Happy Wanderer'®, 'Hobby', 'Cécile Brunner', 'Amsterdam' and 'Wee Jock'®. Every second or third year I pull them out of their pots, give roots a trim, then place fresh potting mix around them as I put them back into their pots. As stated above, patio roses are good for tubs, but you can use many of the small and medium hybrid teas or floribundas if you wish.

Tips for growing roses in containers:

1. Plants in pots dry out faster than those in the ground, so water them more often than plants in beds.

2. Watering leaches nutrients out faster, so maintain regular feeding; that is, one handful of rose fertiliser per month.

3. Do not use soil from the garden— since it cakes hard and can prevent good root development, nor does it drain well. Buy tree and shrub potting mix or make your own.

4. Always leave a 25 mm space below the top of the container when filling with potting mix. This allows water to pool

then soak into the mix.

5   Make sure there are drainage holes at the base of the container. Cover these with broken pots or crockery or large stones, then a small amount of gravel and fill the container with shrub mix.

6   Roses need a minimum tub size of 300 mm deep and 250 mm wide.

7   Containers are versatile as you can move them around.

INDEX

The page numbers in **bold** type indicate illustrations.